CW00497985

Cristiano Ronaldo

By United Library

https://campsite.bio/unitedlibrary

Table of Contents

Introduction

Do you want to read the incredible story of Cristiano Ronaldo?

Cristiano Ronaldo is one of the most famous and successful soccer players in the world. He has an amazing story of overcoming adversity to achieve his goals. This book tells his complete story - from growing up poor in Portugal to becoming one of the richest and most famous athletes on the planet.

Cristiano Ronaldo was born on February 5, 1985, in the Portuguese island of Madeira. Growing up in a poor, single-parent home, Ronaldo developed a strong work ethic early on in life. When he was just eight years old, he began playing for a local youth team, and it quickly became apparent that he had exceptional talent. At age 12, Ronaldo was signed by Lisbon-based club Sporting CP, and he soon rose through the ranks to become one of their most promising young players. In 2003, at age 18, Ronaldo made his debut for Portugal's national team.

The following year, he caught the attention of global soccer powerhouse Real Madrid with a string of impressive performances at the UEFA European Championship. Madrid paid a then-record fee of €94 million to sign Ronaldo from Sporting CP in 2009. Since joining Real Madrid, Ronaldo has established himself as one of the greatest soccer players of all time. He has won five Ballon d'Or awards (an annual prize given to the world's best player), four European Golden Shoe awards (given to the top scorer in Europe), and numerous other honors. In 2018, he joined Italian club Juventus FC in a deal worth over €100 million.

You will learn everything about Ronaldo's life and career in this book. It is a fascinating read that will keep you entertained from beginning to end. You won't be able to put it down!

Cristiano Ronaldo

Cristiano Ronaldo dos Santos Aveiro (Funchal, Madeira; February 5, 1985), better known as **Cristiano Ronaldo** or **CR7**, is a Portuguese footballer who plays as a striker for Manchester United Football Club of England's Premier League and the Portugal national team, of which he is its captain and all-time leading scorer.

Usually identified in the media with the number *CR7*, he is often considered the best and most complete footballer and goal scorer in the world and one of the best of all time, by a large number of people and press linked to the sport, as well as one of the most media figures of his generation. He is, with 813 goals, the top scorer in the history of professional soccer, and with 450, the top scorer in the history of Real Madrid Club de Fútbol, achieving it in the nine seasons he played in this club. He is also, according to the Rec.Sport.Soccer Statistics Foundation (RSSSF) and the International Federation of Football History and Statistics (IFFHS), the third highest scorer in the European First Division championships, with 497 goals -same record worldwide-. The data is recognized by UEFA and FIFA.

Throughout his professional career, he has managed to break several records. Among them, he is the first player to win four Golden Boots, the second player in history to win the Ballon d'Or (with five) -three Ballons d'Or and two FIFA Ballons d'Or-, the first to win FIFA's The Best award for the best player in the world -and the most successful with two along with Robert

Lewandowski-, the top scorer in history for the Portuguese national team (117), the world's top scorer at national team level, and the all-time top scorer in the Champions League (141) counting the qualifying round, a competition in which he also holds the marks for most goals in an edition of the tournament -17 goals in 11 matches (2013-14)-, most goals in a group stage of the tournament -11 goals in six matches (2015-16)- and most times top scorer of the tournament with seven editions. He is also the Madrid player who needed the fewest games (92) to reach 100 goals in the national league championship and the player who needed the fewest games (140) to reach 150 goals in the history of La Liga, the first player in the history of the competition to score against all the teams he faced in a season, the only player capable of scoring in six consecutive Clásicos, and the only one to score in six consecutive visits to Camp Nou, a stadium of maximum rivalry for the Whites.

His consecration as an elite footballer came during his time at Manchester United Football Club, where after winning three *Premier Leagues*, two *EFL Cups*, one *FA Cup*, two *Community Shields*, one Champions League and one Club World Cup, he was awarded the Golden Ball, the *FIFA World Player* and the Golden Shoe, trophies that accredited him as the best footballer in the world as of 2008.

After starring in the most expensive transfer in the history of soccer at the time, he joined Real Madrid Club de Fútbol, where he improved as a footballer, reaching his highest records in play and goals. At the Spanish club he was the first player to surpass the historic figure of thirty-eight goals in a league season, setting the new record at forty goals, a record that helped him win his second Golden Boot in 2011. As a Madrid player, he won two King's Cups, two Leagues, and two Spanish Super Cups, thus completing the Spanish triple crown, plus four Champions Leagues, three European Super Cups and three Club World Cups. His performances led him to conquer another four Ballon d'Or -in 2013, 2014, 2016 and 2017- and another two Golden Boots -in 2014 and 2015- and to rank among the three best players in the world for eight seasons. He is the player who has won the UEFA Best Player Award in Europe the most times, with three titles.

A full international with the Portuguese national team since 2003, he has played in five European Championships, four World Cups, one Confederations Cup and two Nations Leagues, where his greatest achievements were the title wins in Euro 2016 and the 2018-19 Nations League. As for the World Cup and the Confederations Cup, a fourth place in Germany 2006 and a third place in Russia 2017 respectively were his best performances. He is one of the players who are members of the *FIFA Century Club*, made up of those players with more than 100 caps for their national team. His 186 appearances place him third on the list as of 2022 - the most in Portugal's history - and first at UEFA level.

On December 14, 2020, he was included as a left winger in the first historic Ballon d'Or *Dream Team* and on December 27 of the same year he was voted the best Player of the 21st Century.

Since 2014, he has been a Grand Officer of the Order of Infante Don Enrique, one of the highest recognitions granted in Portugal, for his relevant services granted to his country, as well as his cultural, historical and values expansion.

In 2020, he had $105 million, making him soccer's first billionaire.

In 2021 it had $120 million.

Childhood and beginnings

Cristiano Ronaldo dos Santos Aveiro was born in São Pedro, Funchal, on the Portuguese island of Madeira, and grew up in the Santo António area, one of Portugal's poorest neighborhoods. He is the fourth and youngest child of the marriage between Maria Dolores dos Santos Viveiros (b. 1953), a cook, and José Dinis Aveiro (1954-2005), a municipal gardener and utilityman. His paternal great-grandmother, Isabel da Piedade, was from the island of São Vicente, Cape Verde. He has an older brother, Hugo (b. 1975) and two older sisters, Elma (b. 1973) and Liliana Cátia "Katia" (b. 1977), who is a singer. His mother revealed that when she was pregnant with him she wanted to abort him, due to his father's alcohol addiction, the family's poor economic situation and because she already had too many children. However, his doctor refused to perform the procedure. Cristiano grew up in a Catholic family and in a poor home, sleeping in the same room with all his siblings.

He began to stand out among his teammates at Andorinha, his first club, where his father worked as a tool boy. His idols were his compatriots Rui Costa, Fernando Couto and Luís Figo. When he was ten years old, the big Madeira teams, C. S. Marítimo and C. D. Nacional, were already interested in signing him. D. Nacional, were already interested in signing him. He finally joined Nacional, where he continued his progression, becoming one of the brightest promises of

Portuguese soccer. In 1997, he had a three-day trial to join Sporting Clube de Portugal and finally left C. D. Nacional to join the club in Lisbon, the Portuguese capital, having to move on his own and away from his family. Cristiano would comment years later that this was one of the most difficult decisions of his life, but it was worth it for his soccer career. At that time, C. D. Nacional had a debt of 450,000 escudos, which was paid off thanks to Ronaldo's progression and trajectory during his transfer to Lisbon.

Once the transfer was completed, he began his new journey in the discipline of the Lisbon club starting in the 1997-98 season. In the youth academy directed by Leonardo Véliz, he was assigned, along with the rest of his teammates -among them Ricardo Quaresma and Hugo Viana-, psychologists, personalized tutors who guided him in his studies and doctors who observed his physical growth, which contributed to his formation as a person and footballer. When he was fifteen years old, he was diagnosed with a heart problem that could have forced him to retire from playing soccer. Sporting Lisbon informed his mother about the problem, who, aware of the risks, gave him permission to go to the hospital. He then underwent an operation in which the area of the heart that was causing the problem was analyzed through laser surgery. The surgery was performed in the morning and Cristiano was discharged from the hospital the same afternoon and a few days later he returned to training without any problems.

Club careers

Sporting C. P.

His great soccer development led him to play his first minutes as a professional when he was 17 years old, in the UEFA Champions League qualifier against Inter Milan on August 14, 2002. His First Division debut came on September 30 against Sporting Clube de Braga in a 4-2 defeat. However, in his second league match against Moreirense on October 7, Cristiano scored two goals in a 3-0 win that impressed fans and press alike, making him a regular in Sporting's first team. With his goal, he became the youngest goal scorer in Sporting's history, at 17 years and 8 months. He also became the first player to play in one season in Sporting's youth team, the reserve team and the first team.

In 2002, he came close to signing for Juventus in an exchange for Chilean Marcelo Salas, but the latter declined to play in Portuguese soccer. He was first watched by Liverpool manager Gérard Houllier, but he refused to sign him because he was considered too young and had yet to develop his skills further. However, in the summer of 2003, Sporting and Manchester United played a friendly match on the occasion of the inauguration of the José Alvalade Stadium for Euro 2004. In that match, the young winger put in a magnificent performance that would astonish both the opposing players themselves and their manager Alex Ferguson, who secured the Portuguese's transfer to the English club shortly after that same summer.

Manchester United F. C.

Development and breakthrough in England (2003-2007)

For the 2003-04 season, Ronaldo became the first Portuguese player in Manchester United's history. Ronaldo signed a 5-year contract with the club for €12 million, making him the most expensive transfer for a youth player in the history of English soccer at the time. Despite having asked for the number 28, the number he had worn for Sporting Portugal, manager Sir Alex Ferguson gave him the number 7 shirt that had been left by former Manchester United captain David Beckham and used by club legends George Best and Éric Cantona, and using the number 7 served as an extra motivation for Ronaldo. Wearing the number 7 served as an extra motivation for Ronaldo, and a key element in his development in England was his manager, Ferguson, whom he described years later as his "footballing father" and "one of the most important people in my career". Mike Phelan, Ferguson's assistant for years, commented in an interview that they had to transform Cristiano from an individualistic player to a team player, demanding hard training that the Portuguese accepted and followed to perfection.

He made his Premier League debut on August 16, 2003, against Bolton Wanderers, coming on in the 60th minute for England midfielder Nicky Butt. He received a standing ovation when he came on, and his performance was widely acclaimed by George Best, describing it as "the most exciting debut I've seen in years". He scored his first goal from a direct free-kick in a 3-0 win over Portsmouth on November 1 at Old Trafford. He scored three more goals in the second half of the season, the last coming on the final day of the league against Aston Villa, a game in which he also received the first red card of his career. Ronaldo ended his first season in England by winning the FA Cup with a 3-0 win over Millwall of England's League One third tier in Cardiff; Ronaldo opened the scoring and was named man of the match. However, the British press was critical of Cristiano during the season for his "overly elaborate" dribbling when attempting to dribble past an opponent, but teammate Gary Neville said he was "not a show pony, but the real thing," and predicted he would become a world-class player.

During the start of 2005, Ronaldo played two of his best games of the 2004-05 season, producing a goal and an assist against Aston Villa and a brace against title rivals Arsenal. He played the full 120 minutes in the 2004-05 FA Cup final against Arsenal, which ended in a goalless draw, and scored his chance in the penalty shootout that ended in defeat. Ronaldo scored Manchester United's 1000th Premier League goal in a 4-1 loss to Middlesbrough. During the middle of the season, in November, he signed a new contract extending his previous deal for two more years until 2010. Ronaldo won his second English title, the League Cup, after scoring the third goal in United's 4-0 win over Wigan Athletic.

In his third season in England, Ronaldo was involved in several incidents. He was suspended for one match by

UEFA for "giving the finger" to Benfica fans, and was sent off in the Manchester derby when he fouled City's Andy Cole. During this season he also had several problems with teammate Ruud van Nistelrooy, who criticized the Portuguese's way of playing. In the 2006 World Cup in Germany, in a clash between Portugal and England, after a foul involving teammate Wayne Rooney, Cristiano demanded the referee to send the English striker out of the match. This led to England's defeat, and subsequently to booing by United fans towards Ronaldo, who publicly asked to be transferred, regretting the little support he had from the club after the incident. However, United denied the possibility of him leaving the club.

Despite the altercation, the 2006-07 season would be Cristiano's definitive emergence in the team, breaking the 20-goal barrier and winning the Premier League for the first time. A key part of his growth was his personal training with team trainer René Meulensteen, who taught him to be more unpredictable, improve his team play and capitalize on his scoring chances rather than waiting for the opportunity to score the aesthetic goals he was already known for. He scored three straight braces in late December, against Aston Villa (an important win that took United to the top of the table), Wigan, and Reading, which led to his being named Barclays Premier League Player of the Month in November and December, only the third player to receive back-to-back honors.

Establishment as the world's best player and conquest of Europe (2007-08)

In the quarterfinals of the 2006-07 UEFA Champions League, Ronaldo scored his first goals in his 30th appearance in the competition, finding the net twice in a 7-1 win over Roma. He would go on to score in the first leg of the semifinals against Milan in just four minutes of the match, which would end in a 3-2 victory, although he would later be eliminated in the second leg after a 3-0 defeat at the San Siro. He also helped United reach the FA Cup final, but the deciding match against Chelsea ended in a 1-0 defeat. Cristiano scored the only goal in the Manchester derby on 5 May 2007 (his 50th goal for the club), the day Manchester United claimed their first Premier League title after a four-year drought. As a result of his performances, he was awarded "Player of the Year", "Fans' Favorite Player", and "Young Player of the Year" by the PFA, and "Player of the Year" by the FWA, the first player to win all four awards by the PFA and FWA. He was also awarded by the Portuguese newspaper A Bola as "Portuguese Sportsman of the Year", for his important contribution to the expansion of Portuguese soccer throughout the world. At the same time, his salary at the club was raised to £120,000 euros per week (£31 million in total) as part of a five-year contract extension with United. Ronaldo was named second in the Ballon d'Or voting, behind Kaka, and finished third in the FIFA World Player of the Year award, behind Lionel Messi and Kaka.

On August 5, he added another title to his trophy cabinet by winning the Community Shield with a penalty shootout victory over Chelsea, and after yet another dubious start to the tournament, he extended his goal tally to become United's all-time leading goalscorer in a single season, surpassing the mark of 32 goals set by Northern Ireland's George Best during the 1967-68 season. He scored his first hat-trick of two for Manchester on January 12, 2008 at Newcastle United in a 6-0 win, which took United to the top of the league table. A month later, on March 19, he captained United for the first time in a home win over Bolton, scoring a brace. His 31 league goals earned him the Premier League Golden Shoe for the first time, as well as the European Golden Shoe, making him the first winger to do so, and he also won the PFA and FWA Player of the Year awards for the second consecutive season.

His performances finally took him to a European final on May 21, 2008, when he played in the Champions League final against Chelsea, in the first final between two Premier League teams in the competition. He was the scorer of his club's only goal in the final draw, so the match was decided on penalty kicks. Ronaldo missed, but despite this, mistakes by rival defender John Terry and French striker Nicolas Anelka gave him his first continental title. He was named player of the tournament and also the tournament's top scorer. At the end of the campaign, Cristiano Ronaldo scored 42 goals, 31 of them in the league - a result that left him two goals short of surpassing the performance of Dutch striker Ruud Van Nistelrooy in the 2002-03 season - and was proclaimed winner of another Community Shield despite missing out due to injury.

During the summer of 2008, there was speculation about the player's possible departure to Real Madrid C. F., the club that had always shown the greatest interest in the player. However, negotiations were postponed until the following season when a pre-contract was signed in December 2008. United filed a manipulation complaint with FIFA's governing body over Madrid's alleged pursuit of their player, but they refused to take action. FIFA president Sepp Blatter said the player should be allowed to leave his club, describing the situation as "modern slavery." Despite Ronaldo publicly agreeing with Blatter, he remained at United for another year.

Last season in England and continued success (2008-09)

With the 2008-09 season ahead of him, Ronaldo suffered an ankle injury that would keep him off the field until October. His recovery came early, and he scored his 100th goal for United in all competitions, a free-kick double in a 5-0 win over Stoke City on November 15, which meant he had now scored against all 19 Premier League teams. At the close of 2008 he won the Club World Cup for Liga de Quito, being named the tournament's second best player behind teammate Wayne Rooney. He was awarded the FIFA World Player, the Golden Eleven and the Golden Ball, an award that had not been won by a player of the Manchester team for 40 years.

He scored one of the most beautiful goals of his career in the Champions League match against his old rival Porto, scoring from over thirty-five meters. The goal was later awarded the Puskás Award for the best goal of the year. His high performance led the club to its second consecutive Champions League final. In it they were defeated by F. C. Barcelona by 2-0, although they were able to retain the Premier League title. He finished the season with a record of 54 appearances and 24 goals for United, and with a total record of 118 goals in 292 games.

Real Madrid C. F.

Most expensive transfer in history and first year in Spain (2009-2010)

On June 11, 2009, the English club accepted Real Madrid's £80 million bid , confirming two weeks later that it was the most expensive transfer in soccer history to date - second only to Neymar's 222 million euro move from FC Barcelona to PSG. Nearly 80,000 thousand people attended the presentation ceremony, breaking Diego Maradona's 25-year-old record when he was presented at Napoli in front of 75 thousand fans. As club captain Raúl already had the number 7, Cristiano was assigned the number 9, which was presented by Madrid legend Alfredo Di Stéfano.

He made his debut on July 21 against Irish side Shamrock Rovers during pre-season, and scored his first goals in white in the 2009 Peace Cup against Ecuador's Liga de Quito and Juventus. His official debuts came in a La Liga match against Deportivo La Coruña, where he scored a goal in his team's 3-2 win, and in a Champions League match against Zürich, where he scored twice in a 2-5 win. He scored in his first four games for the club, the first player in Madrid history to do so. His strong start to the campaign was interrupted by an injury in October while with the Portuguese national team, which kept him out for seven weeks. A week after his return, he was sent off for the first time in Spain, against Almeria. Midway through the season, he came second in the voting for the Ballon d'Or, losing out to Lionel Messi, another young star who was emerging from Madrid's eternal rivals, F.C Barcelona, and who would be his main competitor during his years in Spain.

His records continued to increase and he scored his first hat-trick for Real Madrid on May 5, 2010 against Mallorca. However, despite his great performances in which he scored 33 goals in 35 games played, being the team's top scorer, the club was unable to win any titles. Ronaldo's best goal-scoring average, at almost a goal per game, was not enough to overcome the round of 16 of the Champions League, nor the round of 32 of the Copa del Rey -in which he could not make his debut due to injury-, where the club suffered two painful eliminations in two competitions in which it was plunged into a results crisis after several seasons of early or crucial eliminations.

Under Mourinho: League champion and scoring records (2010-2013)

With the departure of captain Raúl, Ronaldo inherited his classic dorsal number "7", with which he would have a spectacular start to the season in which he stood out as one of the best goal scorers ever seen. Among his performances, the one against Racing Santander, where he scored for the first time in his career four goals in one game, or the ones that took place in October, where he scored in 6 consecutive games a total of 13 goals, the most in a calendar month for him, stood out. By early December, his progression seemed not to end and he scored more than 20 goals in less than 20 games in all competitions, ending 2010 with the best record of his career, 48 goals in total, which was 13 more than he achieved in 2008 with Manchester United. However, despite his incredible numbers, he failed to make the podium for the inaugural FIFA Ballon d'Or. On March 3, in the match against Malaga, the player scored his fifth hat-trick of the season, shattering his records at the English club, where he was only able to score one in six years.

During a historic run of four Clasicos in 2011, in which there was a great media clash between the coaches of the two clubs, with Madrid's Jose Mourinho representing the school of counter-attacking and defensive discipline, and Barcelona's Pep Guardiola leaning more towards attacking and touch soccer, the press and fans also had high expectations for the rivalry between Cristiano, who came across as a more individualistic and selfish player, and Messi, who was seen more as a team player with a low profile. Despite failing to score in Madrid's Champions League semifinal elimination, Cristiano did manage to equalize in the La Liga match and scored a historic header in extra time in the final of the Copa del Rey to win his first title with Real Madrid.

His records increased with a spectacular end of La Liga, where he scored another hat-trick against Sevilla away from home, another hat-trick against Getafe, and four more in total in two other games that would leave his personal record at 40 goals, surpassing Hugo Sánchez and Telmo Zarra's all-time record of 38 in a league season. Even so, the championship would end up being won by Barcelona. He finished the season with 53 goals in 54 games in all competition, a record he shared with Argentine Lionel Messi. In addition to winning the Pichichi Trophy, Cristiano won the Golden Shoe for the second time, becoming the only player to win the award playing in two different leagues.

In the following season, 2011-12, Ronaldo surpassed his own previously achieved records by reaching 60 goals in all competitions, his personal best. He regained a place on the 2011 Ballon d'Or podium, as second behind Messi, after scoring hat-tricks against Real Zaragoza, Rayo Vallecano, Malaga, Osasuna, and Sevilla, with the latter depositing Madrid at the top of the La Liga table for half the season. He finished 2011 with 20 goals in La Liga, 15 of them spread over 5 hat-tricks. His goals did not stop, and he started 2012 by scoring a goal in the first leg of the Copa del Rey quarterfinals against Barcelona, and repeated in the second leg, thus starting a historic scoring streak against the "culés", which continued on April 21 in La Liga, when his goal at the Camp Nou practically sentenced the League in favor of the Whites after a 1-2 victory. Three days later, he scored a brace in the second leg of the Champions League semifinals against Bayern Munich, however, due to the result of the first leg, the final was decided by penalties, where the German team won, depriving him of his third final in Europe's top club competition. However, his goals did help the club to win the league title on May 2 after beating Athletic Club 3-0 at the San Mamés stadium, in Madrid's famous "League of records", breaking the 100-point mark and setting a record of 121 goals, in what was the club's first after a four-year drought. With his 46 goals in the domestic championship, he became the first player in history to score 40 goals or more in two consecutive La Liga seasons, in addition to scoring against all the teams he faced in La Liga that season, the first player in the history of the competition to do so.

He began the 2012-13 season by scoring in the first leg of the Spanish Super Cup against Barcelona at Camp Nou, becoming the only Madrid player in history to score in four consecutive visits to the Barcelona ground.In the second leg, in which he won the Super Cup title, the Portuguese player scored again, thus equaling the record of the Chilean Iván Zamorano, the only player so far capable of scoring in five consecutive "Clásicos", which he surpassed on October 7 when he scored a brace against the Catalans in La Liga to surpass the South American's record and score for the sixth consecutive clásico, something that no one had ever done before. Despite Ronaldo's public comments that he was unhappy due to a "personal problem" with the club, which he demonstrated when he decided not to celebrate his 150th goal for Madrid, his goalscoring record did not suffer. After scoring a hat-trick, including two penalties, against Deportivo La Coruña, Cristiano scored his first Champions League hat-trick in a 4-1 win over Ajax. His performances again placed him second in the 2012 Ballon d'Or, an award that ended up being won by Messi for the fourth consecutive time.

After the winter break for the season, Ronaldo captained Real Madrid for the first time in an official match, scoring a brace in a hard-fought 4-3 win over Real Sociedad on January 6. Shortly after, he became the first non-Spanish player in 60 years to captain the club during El Clasico on January 30, 2013, a match that also marked his 500th appearance at club level. Three days later, he reached 300 goals overall after scoring a perfect hat-trick against Getafe. Cristiano would help Real Madrid reach the 2013 Copa del Rey final after scoring a brace in El Clasico in the semifinals, which marked his sixth consecutive game at Camp Nou where he scored, a club record. In the final, he scored the opening goal of the match with a header in what would be a 2-1 loss to Atletico Madrid, a match in which he would also be sent off for violent conduct. In the round of 16 of the Champions League, Cristiano faced Manchester United for the first time. After scoring the 1-1 goal at the Santiago Bernabeu, with a header where he jumped almost 3 meters, in the second leg he scored the winning goal for 2-1 in his return to Old Trafford. He did not celebrate any of the goals he scored out of respect for his former club. After scoring three goals against Galatasaray in the quarterfinals, Ronaldo scored Madrid's only goal in the 4-1 loss to Borussia Dortmund in the first leg of the semifinals, which would eventually lead to the Madrid side's eventual elimination, winning the second leg 2-0 but crashing out of the competition in the semifinals for the third consecutive year.

With Ancelotti: *La Décima* and two consecutive Ballon d'Or awards (2013-2015).

After a disappointing season without titles, Mourinho would end up being dismissed from his position as coach, being replaced by the historic Italian manager Carlo Ancelotti. On September 15, 2013, his renewal with the club was announced, extending his contract until the end of the 2017-18 season, with a salary of 17 million euros net, making him the highest paid footballer in the world.For the start of the 2013-14 season, the club signed winger Gareth Bale, who in his transfer surpassed Ronaldo's record as the most expensive signing in history, with the Welshman being paid over €100 million. Together with French striker Karim Benzema, the three forwards formed a *trident* popularized as the "BBC", an acronym for Bale, Benzema and Cristiano. CR7 scored 32 goals in 22 games played for club and country by mid-November 2013, including five hat-tricks. The Portuguese closed 2013 with 69 goals in 59 appearances, his highest tally at the end of a year, and won his second Ballon d'Or after four years, and his first since the merger of the Ballon d'Or and FIFA World Player of the Year trophies.

With his individual achievements, Cristiano would finally achieve success with Real Madrid after winning *La Décima*, the tenth Champions League trophy for Real Madrid, an achievement the club had been denied for 12 years. His goal in the 3-0 win over Borussia Dortmund (his 100th Champions League match) was his 14th goal in the competition, breaking the record

Messi had set two years earlier. After scoring a brace in the historic 4-0 thrashing of Bayern Munich (coached by Guardiola) in Germany, Ronaldo scored the last goal in extra time in the final against Atlético de Madrid in Lisbon, becoming the only player to score in two victorious European Cup finals with two different teams. In that edition, Cristiano would become the all-time top scorer in an edition of the Champions League with 17 goals. His overall performance was held back by patellar tendonitis and a torn hamstring, which bothered him in the final months of the campaign. Ronaldo played in the final despite medical advice not to, with the player commenting that "in life you don't win without sacrifices, that's why you have to take risks."

In the Copa del Rey he helped the team reach the final after scoring two penalties against Atlético de Madrid at the Vicente Calderón, which meant that Ronaldo managed to score in every minute of the 90 minutes of a regular match. His injury problems prevented him from being present in the final victory over Barcelona. In La Liga, the Portuguese would score 31 goals in 30 games, winning the Pichichi and his third Golden Shoe, this time together with Luis Suarez. A back-heel volley goal against Valencia was recognized as the best goal of the Professional Football League, who also named him the best player of La Liga that year.

During his 2014-15 season, Ronaldo set a new personal best by scoring 61 goals in all competitions, as well as making his best scoring start in La Liga with 15 goals in the first eight games. His 23rd La Liga hat-trick against Celta Vigo on September 6, 2015 made him the fastest player to reach 200 goals in Spain's Primera División, having only achieved the landmark in his

178th game. After winning the Club World Cup against San Lorenzo, Cristiano won his second consecutive Ballon d'Or, joining Johan Cruyff, Michel Platini and Marco van Basten on the list of three-time winners of the award. Two days later, the Portuguese Football Federation presented him with the "Quina de Ouro", accrediting him as the best Portuguese footballer in history, ahead of Eusébio and Luis Figo.

All-time leading scorer and three-time Champions League winner (2015-2018).

Madrid finished second in La Liga, and was eliminated in the Champions League semifinals against Juventus. In La Liga, he scored five career goals for the first time, including a hat-trick in eight minutes, in a 9-1 win over Granada. He scored his 300th goal for his club just three days later in a 2-0 win over Rayo Vallecano. Several hat-tricks in a row, including against Sevilla, Espanyol and Getafe took his hat-trick tally to 31, surpassing Di Stéfano's record of 28. Cristiano would finish that season with 48 goals, winning his second consecutive Pichichi and his record fourth Golden Boot.

For the 2015-16 season, Ancelotti would end up dismissed from his position after failing to achieve the objectives, and would be replaced by Rafa Benítez. This would be the season that Ronaldo would be consecrated as Real Madrid's all-time top scorer, first in La Liga and then in all competitions. On September 12, he scored five goals against Espanyol, surpassing Raul's record of 230 goals in La Liga. A month later, on October 17, he again surpassed Raul when he scored the second goal against Levante to surpass his all-time total of 324 goals. Ronaldo also became the all-time leading scorer in the Champions League after scoring a hat-trick against Shaktar Donetsk. He also reached 500 goals for club and country on September 30 after a brace against Malmo.

Despite continuing to set records, Madrid would have a dismal start to the league, with Rafa Benítez being dismissed from his post in January, and being replaced by the legend Zinedine Zidane, who was coaching Castilla. Following those records, Cristiano became the second top scorer in the history of the Spanish league championship on March 5, 2016 after surpassing the 250 goals scored by Telmo Zarra, behind Messi. In the European play-off against VfL Wolfsburg, played in April, he was key as he scored a hat-trick in the second leg, after losing the first leg 2-0, thus reaching 15 goals in the quarterfinals of the competition, surpassing Alfredo Di Stéfano's record, which stood at 14. Thanks to his hat-trick, he became the top scorer of the edition for the fourth consecutive time, and his fifth in total. However, Ronaldo would have a much-criticized final against Atlético de Madrid, despite scoring the final penalty for Madrid's victory, who won their eleventh Champions League. For the sixth consecutive year, he finished the season scoring more than 50 goals. For his efforts during the season, he won the European Player of the Year award for the second time.

For the 2016-17 season, Cristiano had just returned from winning the first international title in Portugal's history, but in the final against France he had suffered an injury, so he missed the European Super Cup against Sevilla. In La Liga, he became the top scorer in the history of the Madrid derby after scoring a hat-trick against Atleti, with 18 goals. On December 15, he reached 500 goals at club level, after scoring against América in the Club World Cup. In the final of the tournament, he scored a hat-trick against Kashima Antlers for a 4-2 victory, which led him to finish as the tournament's top scorer and best player. By early 2017, he would win his fifth Ballon d'Or, and the first FIFA The Best, a resurrection of the former FIFA World Player of the Year.

In the 2016-17 Champions League, Cristiano would reach one of the best form of his career. In the first leg of the quarterfinals against Bayern Munich, after Madrid started losing, Cristiano would score a brace to put Madrid ahead in the series. In the second leg, the Germans would take the match to extra time, where Cristiano would finish off the match with a perfect hat-trick, which would also bring him to 100 goals in the competition. In the quarterfinals, another Madrid derby would be replayed against Atlético de Madrid. Cristiano would have an outstanding match, dispatching Cholo Simeone's team with another hat-trick. In the final against Juventus, CR7 would open the scoring, and then score the third goal in Madrid's 4-1 win over the Italians, to close his participation with twelve goals, the fifth consecutive time he surpassed the ten-goal mark in the competition and was proclaimed top scorer, the first and only player to achieve both records to date.Under the new format, he became the first player to score in three finals, surpassed in the European Cup history (counting editions under the old format) only by Alfredo Di Stéfano, who scored in five finals.

On May 14, he reached 400 goals with the Merengue club, and surpassed them shortly after when he scored a brace against Sevilla in La Liga. Previously, the player became the all-time top scorer in the five best leagues in Europe, surpassing the previous record of Englishman Jimmy Greaves of 366 goals dating back to 1971, a mark he later raised to 373 goals. That same month, he was crowned La Liga champion again, the club's first since 2012, beating Málaga, playing 29 games and scoring 25 goals.

In the 2017-18 season, Ronaldo scored a stunning goal from outside the box in the 3-1 victory over Barcelona in the first leg of the Spanish Super Cup, which would end in an expulsion by the Portuguese after an alleged aggression to the referee, and a new trophy for Madrid. On October 23, he won his second The Best award. On December 6, he became the first player to score in all six Champions League group stage matches. A week later, he scored a free-kick goal in Real Madrid's Club World Cup final win over Gremio. On March 3, he reached 300 goals in La Liga after 286 games, making him the fastest player to reach that mark and only the second player to do so after Messi. On March 18, he reached his 50th hat-trick, scoring four goals against Girona.

On April 3, Cristiano scored the first two goals in the 3-0 victory over Juventus in the Champions League quarterfinals, the second goal being a "Chilean". Described as a "Playstation" goal by Juventus defender Andrea Barzagli, and one of the best in the history of the tournament, the entire stadium gave the Portuguese a standing ovation, including players and coaches. In the second leg of the series, he scored the decisive penalty in extra time to send Madrid through to the semifinals, after trailing 3-0, with a 4-3 aggregate victory. It was also his tenth goal against Juventus in the Champions League, a record in the competition. In the final, Real Madrid defeated Liverpool 3-1, marking the fifth Champions League for Cristiano in his overall record, and the thirteenth for the club. He finished as the edition's top scorer for the sixth consecutive time, ending the campaign with 15 goals. In a press conference after the match, Cristiano hinted that he could have ended his time at the club after being crowned three-time European Cup winner. He ended his interview with his characteristic celebratory shout.

Juventus F. C.

Adaptation and first Serie A title (2018-19).

Despite months of negotiating a new contract with Real Madrid, on July 10, 2018 Cristiano signed a four-year contract with Italy's Juventus after completing a €100 million transfer, which included an additional €12 million for bonuses and training rights. The transfer was the highest transfer made by a player over the age of 30, and the most expensive made by an Italian team. Since his signing, Ronaldo confessed that he needed a new challenge as a fundamental reason for leaving Madrid, but later attributed the transfer to the lack of support he felt was shown by Real Madrid president Florentino Perez.

On August 18, Cristiano made his official debut for Juventus in a 3-2 win over Chievo Verona. On September 16, he scored his first two goals for Juventus in a 2-1 win over Sassuolo, his fourth appearance for La *Vecchia Signora*; his second goal was his 400th overall. On September 19, in his first Champions League match for Juventus, he was sent off after 29 minutes for "violent conduct", his first red card in 154 appearances in the competition. Ronaldo left the field in tears. However, the team won 1-0 against Valencia to secure a place in the round of 16, Ronaldo's 100th win in the competition. In December, he scored his 10th Serie A goal of the season from the penalty spot in a 3-0 win over Fiorentina; with this goal, Ronaldo became the first player since John Charles in 1957 to score 10 goals in his first 14 league games for his club. After being voted second in the UEFA Best Player in Europe and The Best awards for the first time in three years, behind Luka Modrić, Cristiano's performances in 2018 also placed him second in the Ballon d'Or, again finishing behind his former Real Madrid teammate.

On January 16, 2019, Ronaldo won his first title with the club, the 2018 Italian Super Cup, after he scored the only match-winning goal against Milan. On February 10, Ronaldo scored in a 3-0 away win over Sassuolo; the ninth consecutive game he scored for Juventus for the league, which saw him equal Giuseppe Signori's record for most away games with at least one goal scored in a single Serie A season. On March 12, Ronaldo had one of his most iconic moments in the Champions League, when he scored a home hat-trick against Atletico Madrid to come from 2-0 down in the first leg of the round of 16. The following month, Ronaldo scored his 125th goal in the competition, opening the scoring in a 1-1 draw in the first leg of Juventus' quarter-final against Ajax. In the second match of the series in Turin, Ronaldo again opened the scoring to give Juventus the lead, but they would go on to lose the match 2-1 and be eliminated from the competition. On April 20, Ronaldo played in the decisive match for the *scudetto* against Fiorentina, which would see Juventus crowned champions of Italy for the eighth consecutive time, winning the match 2-1.On April 27, he scored his 600th overall club goal, a 1-1 draw in the *Derby d'Italia* against classic Inter Milan. Finishing his first Serie A campaign with 21 goals and 8 assists, Ronaldo was voted Serie A's Most Valuable Player.

Second Serie A title (2019-20)

His second season with the *Bianconeri* was marked by the COVID19 pandemic, which led to a stoppage of all competitions between March and June 2020. During the stoppage, Cristiano Ronaldo accepted a 12% reduction in his salary (€3.8 million on his total salary of €31 million), as a measure to deal with the economic consequences of the soccer stoppage on clubs. On the sporting front, the Portuguese managed to win his second *scudetto* and compete, with his 31 goals, against Italy's Ciro Immobile (36) and Poland's Robert Lewandowski (34) until the last day for the Golden Boot. During the campaign, he became the first player to score more than 50 goals in three of the world's major soccer competitions: Italian Serie A, Spanish LaLiga and the English Premier League. Despite the sporting achievements, his team lost the Supercoppa Italiana 1-3 to Lazio, lost to Napoli on penalties in the Coppa final and was eliminated in the round of 16 of the Champions League by Olympique Lyon, which would be the first time since 2010 that Ronaldo failed to advance beyond that round of the competition.

100 goals with Juventus, *Capocannoniere* and Coppa Italia (2020-21)

On September 20, 2020, Ronaldo scored in Juventus' first game of the season, a 3-0 home win over Sampdoria in Serie A. On November 1, after Ronaldo took nearly three weeks to recover from COVID-19, he returned to action against Spezia, where he came off the bench in the second half and scored in the first three minutes. He later scored a second goal from the penalty spot in an eventual 4-1 away win. On December 2, he scored a goal against Dynamo Kiev in a Champions League group stage match to reach his 750th career goal. Ronaldo played his 100th game in all competitions for Juventus on December 13, scoring two penalties in a 3-1 win over Genoa in the league to take his goal tally to 79. On January 20, 2021, Juventus won the 2020 Supercoppa Italiana after a 2-0 win over Napoli, with Ronaldo scoring the opening goal. On March 2, he scored a goal in a 3-0 win over Spezia in his 600th league match to become the first player to score at least 20 goals in each of the last 12 consecutive seasons in Europe's top five leagues. On March 9, Juventus was eliminated from the Champions League in the round of 16 by Porto, again on the away goals rule (4-4 on aggregate). On March 14, he scored the 57th hat-trick of his career in a 3-1 away win over Cagliari.

On May 12, Ronaldo scored in a 3-1 away win over Sassuolo to reach his 100th goal for Juventus in all competitions in his 131st appearance, becoming the fastest Juventus player to achieve the feat. With Juventus' 2-1 victory over Atalanta in the 2021 Coppa Italia final on May 19, Ronaldo became the first player in history to win every major domestic trophy in England, Spain and Italy. Ronaldo finished the league campaign with 29 goals, winning the *Capocannoniere* top scorer award and becoming the first player to finish as top scorer in the English, Spanish and Italian leagues.

Second stint at Manchester United F. C.

Top scorer in soccer history (2021-22)

During the transfer window for the 2021-22 season, Ronaldo made public his intentions to leave Juventus, and the club put him up for sale. In August there were strong rumors about a possible move to Manchester City, in a deal in which his agent, Jorge Mendes, went as far as agreeing a pre-contract. However, a few weeks later, City pulled out of the negotiation, and on August 27 it was confirmed that Manchester United had reached an agreement with Juventus to sign Cristiano, subject to an agreement on personal terms, visa, and medical checks. The transfer was reported to cost an initial €12 million, signing a two-year contract, plus an optional one, and was confirmed on August 31. It was also reported that the likes of Alex Ferguson and Bruno Fernandes were important in convincing the Portuguese to sign for the *Red Devils.*Cristiano was assigned the number 7 shirt, on loan from teammate Edinson Cavani, who switched to 21. It was reported that sales of Ronaldo's shirt in the first 24 hours broke an all-time record after the transfer, surpassing Lionel Messi's move to Paris Saint-Germain.

On September 11, Ronaldo made his second Old Trafford debut, scoring the first two goals in a 4-1 win over Newcastle. On September 29, he scored an agonizing goal against Villareal in the Champions League to win 2-1 at home and surpass Iker Casillas' record as the player with the most appearances in the history of the competition. On December 2, Cristiano scored a brace in a 3-2 home win over Arsenal, taking him over the 800-goal mark for his career. In 2022, he went six games without scoring, something that had not happened since 2010. He scored again on February 15, against Brighton, and on March 12, he scored a hat-trick in a 3-2 win over Tottenham, taking his tally to 807 goals and surpassing Josef Bican as the top scorer in the history of professional soccer. Despite his excellent performance in the Champions League group stage, Ronaldo would end up eliminated in the round of 16 against Atlético Madrid by an aggregate score of 2-1. Ronaldo would finish the 2021-22 season without titles for the first time since the 2009-10 campaign.

National team

Lower categories and first international tournaments (2001-2007)

Ronaldo began his international career with Portugal's U-15 team in 2001. During his career with the youth divisions, Ronaldo represented the U-15, U-20, U-21 and U-23 teams, scoring 38 international caps and 18 goals. He was champion of the 2003 Hopes of Toulon Tournament with the U-21 team.

At the age of 18, Ronaldo made his first appearance for Portugal's senior team in a 1-0 win over Kazakhstan on August 20, 2003, coming on as a halftime substitute for Luis Figo. He was eventually called up for Euro 2004, held in his native country, and scored his first goal in an international team tournament in a 2-1 loss to eventual champions Greece in the group stage. After scoring his chance in the penalty shootout against England in the quarterfinals, Cristiano helped the team reach the final by scoring the first goal in a 2-1 win over the Netherlands. He was included in the Team of the Championship, having made two assists in addition to his two goals in the tournament.

Cristiano was Portugal's second top scorer in its qualifying group for the 2006 World Cup in Germany, with seven goals scored. During the tournament, he scored his first World Cup goal against Iran from the penalty spot in Portugal's second group stage match. At the age of 21 years and 132 days, Ronaldo became the youngest player in the history of the Portuguese national team to score in a World Cup. In the famous Round of 16 match against the Netherlands, known as the Battle of Nuremberg, Ronaldo was forced to leave the field injured after a tackle by Dutch defender Khalid Boulahrouz. After Portugal's 1-0 victory, Cristiano accused Boulahrouz of intentionally trying to injure him, but still ended up recovering in time for the next match. In the quarterfinals against England, Cristiano's Manchester United teammate at the time, Wayne Rooney, was sent off after fouling Portuguese defender Ricardo Caravalho. Although the referee later clarified that the red card was due solely to Rooney's infraction, British tabloids speculated that Ronaldo had influenced his decision by complaining aggressively after he was seen on replays winking at the Portugal bench following Rooney's dismissal. Ronaldo then scored the decisive penalty in the shootout that sent Portugal into the semifinals of the tournament. However, in the semi-final against France, a solitary goal by Zinedine Zidane prevented Ronaldo from reaching his second consecutive final with his national team, in a match where he was also booed by fans. Because of his conduct in the tournament, FIFA ended up giving the Best Young Player of the World Cup award to Lucas Podolski of Germany. After the Cup, Ronaldo continued to represent Portugal in qualifying matches for Euro 2008, scoring two goals in the process.

Assuming the captaincy and difficult years (2007-2012)

A day after his 22nd birthday, Ronaldo captained Portugal for the first time in a friendly against Brazil on February 6, 2007, honoring the request of the president of the Portuguese Football Federation, Carlos Silva, who had died two days earlier. With Euro 2008 ahead of him, Cristiano inherited the number 7 jersey from Luis Figo. Despite scoring 8 goals in the qualifiers, the second highest mark, he could only score one goal in the tournament, the second of Portugal's three goals in their second match against Czech Republic, in which the Portuguese won 3-1. They were finally eliminated in the quarterfinals by Germany, failing to repeat the success of the previous edition.

After Portugal's failure at the European Championship, the Federation fired Luis Felipe Scolari and hired Carlos Queiroz as the new coach, a former assistant to Ferguson at Manchester United. Queiroz made Cristiano the permanent captain of the team in July 2008. Cristiano failed to score a single goal during the entire 2010 World Cup Qualifiers for South Africa, just as Portugal avoided being knocked out of the tournament by winning a playoff against Bosnia. In the World Cup group stage, Cristiano was named man of the match in all three games, against Ivory Coast, North Korea, against whom he scored his only goal of the tournament, and Brazil. Portugal was eventually eliminated by Spain, the eventual champions of the tournament, by just 1-0.

Ronaldo scored seven goals in the qualifiers for Euro 2012, including two braces in the play-off against Bosnia, which sent Portugal to the tournament, where they were placed in the "group of death", along with the Germany of the "Löw Generation", the Netherlands, runners-up in the last World Cup in South Africa, and the dangerous Denmark team. In the last match of the group stage, against the Netherlands, Cristiano secured the victory by scoring a brace for the final 2-1, and against the Czech Republic in the quarterfinals, he scored a header for a 1-0 win, being voted the Most Valuable Player in both matches. After the semifinals against Spain were tied goalless, with Ronaldo sending three shots against the crossbar, Portugal was eliminated on penalties. Cristiano was left without a penalty kick, as he was chosen to take the fifth unused penalty, a decision that was questioned by the media. Ronaldo's own teammate, Nani, said that Cristiano "demanded" to take the last penalty. As joint top scorer with three goals, along with five other players, he was again included in the team of the tournament.

Portugal's all-time leading scorer and European champion (2012-2016).

During the 2014 World Cup Qualifiers, Cristiano scored a total of eight goals. A qualifying match on October 17, 2012, a 1-1 draw against Northern Ireland, marked his 100th appearance for the national team. His first international hat-trick also came against Northern Ireland, when he scored three times in 15 minutes in a 4-2 win on September 6, 2013. After Portugal failed to qualify during the regular qualifiers, Cristiano scored all four of the team's goals in the playoff against Sweden, which was also a clash between Cristiano and Zlatan Ibrahimović, who secured their passage to the competition. His hat-trick in the return leg took his international goal tally to 47, equaling Pauleta's record. Cristiano would eventually score a brace against Cameroon on March 5, 2014 to become his country's all-time leading scorer.

Ronaldo was part of the Portuguese delegation for the World Cup, despite carrying patellar tendonitis and a thigh injury, potentially risking his career. Ronaldo would later comment, "If we had two or three Cristiano Ronaldos in the team, I would feel more comfortable. But we don't have." Despite doubts about his condition, being forced to leave practice twice, Ronaldo played all 90 minutes of the first match against Germany, although he was unable to prevent the 4-0 drubbing. After providing a late assist in the 2-2 draw against the United States, he scored a late winner in the 2-1 victory over Ghana. His 50th international goal made him the first Portuguese player to play and score in three World Cups. Portugal was eliminated early in the group stage on goal difference.

After missing the first Euro 2016 Qualifying match against Albania due to injury, Ronaldo scored an injury time goal in the 95th minute to give Portugal a 1-0 win over Denmark. On November 14, 2014, he played against Armenia also for Euro qualification, where he scored the only goal of the match to give his national team the victory. At the start of the tournament, Ronaldo failed to score in the team's draws against Iceland and Austria, despite having 20 shots on goal, and in the latter, he became the player with the most appearances for Portugal, surpassing Figo, with 128. With a brace scored in the 3-3 draw against Hungary, Ronaldo became the first player to score in four European tournaments, also making 17 appearances, a record. Despite finishing third in their group, behind Hungary and Iceland, the team advanced to the next round due to the new tournament format, still without winning any of their three matches.

In Portugal's first knockout match, Ronaldo's only scoring chance was saved by Croatia goalkeeper Danijel Subašić, but the rebound was tapped in by Ricardo Quaresma, who scored the defining goal in extra time. After the team eliminated Poland on penalties, with Ronaldo scoring the first penalty, he became the first player to participate in three Euro semifinals; he scored the opening goal in the 2-0 win over Wales, equaling Michel Platini's record as the tournament's all-time leading scorer with nine goals. In the final against hosts France, Ronaldo had to leave the field after a foul by Dimitri Payet, and despite multiple treatments and attempts to continue, he was replaced by Quaresma 25 minutes into the match. During extra time, Éder scored the winning goal in the 109th minute. As captain of the team, Cristiano lifted the trophy in celebration of his country's first official title, and also won the tournament's Silver Shoe, scoring three goals and providing three assists.

Post-European and World Championship (2016-2018).

In Portugal's opening match of the 2017 Confederations Cup against Mexico on June 17, Cristiano set up Quaresma's opening goal for the 2-2 final draw. Three days later, he scored the only goal in the win against hosts Russia. On June 24, he scored the penalty goal in the 4-0 win over New Zealand, which allowed Portugal to advance from the group and into the semifinals of the tournament; with his 75th international goal, Ronaldo also equaled Sándor Kocsis as Europe's second all-time leading scorer, behind only Ferenc Puskás. He was named Man of the Match in all three of Portugal's group stage matches. Ronaldo left the competition early; after the team's 3-0 loss to Chile, he was on leave to return home early to witness the birth of his new son, and therefore was not present for Portugal's third-place match, which they beat Mexico 2-1 in extra time.

On 31 August 2017, Ronaldo scored a hat-trick in a 5-1 win over the Faroe Islands in a Russia 2018 World Cup qualifier, which saw him overtake Pelé and equal Hussein Saeed as the fifth highest scorer in international soccer with 78 goals. These goals took his tally in World Cup qualifiers to 14, equaling Predrag Mijatović's record for most goals in a single UEFA qualifying campaign, and also saw him break the record for most goals scored in a European qualifying group, surpassing the previous record of 13 goals scored by David Healy and Robert Lewandowski. Ronaldo's hat-trick took his World Cup qualifying goals total to 29, making him the top scorer in UEFA qualifiers, ahead of Andriy Shevchenko, and the top scorer in World Cup qualifiers and finals combined with 32 goals, ahead of Miroslav Klose. Ronaldo subsequently added to this tally by scoring a goal against Andorra in a 2-0 win.

On June 15, 2018, Ronaldo became the oldest player to score a 'hat-trick' in a World Cup match, helping Portugal secure a 3-3 draw against Spain (his third goal was a 30-yard free kick) in their opening match. In doing so, he became the first Portuguese player to score a goal in four World Cups and one of only four players of any nationality to do so. On June 20, Ronaldo scored the only goal in a 1-0 win over Morocco, breaking Puskás' record as Europe's all-time leading scorer with 85 international goals. In the final group match against Iran on June 25, Ronaldo missed a penalty in an eventual 1-1 draw that saw Portugal advance to the second round as group runners-up behind Spain. On June 30, Portugal was eliminated after a 2-1 loss to Uruguay in the round of 16. For his performances in the tournament, Ronaldo was included in the World Cup All-Star Team.

Nations League and 100 international goals (2018-2020).

After the World Cup, Ronaldo missed six international matches, including the entire 2018-19 UEFA Nations League league phase, but played for Portugal in the Nations League Final Four in June 2019, where they were home. In the semifinals on June 5, he scored a hat-trick against Switzerland to reach the final. In scoring the first goal, he became the first player to score in 10 consecutive international competitions, breaking the record previously shared by Ghana's Asamoah Gyan. In the final of the tournament four days later, Portugal defeated the Netherlands 1-0 to win the second title in its history.

On September 10, 2019, Ronaldo scored four goals in a 5-1 away win over Lithuania in a Euro 2020 qualifier; in the process, he surpassed Robbie Keane (23 goals) as the player with the most goals in Euro qualifying, setting a new record with 25 goals. He also set a new record for goals against most national teams, 40, while completing his eighth international hat-trick. On October 14, he scored his 700th career goal for club and country from the penalty spot in his 974th career appearance, a 2-1 loss to Ukraine in a Euro 2020 qualifier. On November 17, Ronaldo scored his 99th goal in a 2-0 win over Luxembourg, leading Portugal to qualify for Euro 2020. On September 8, 2020, Ronaldo scored his 100th and 101st international goals in a 2-0 away win over Sweden in a 2020-21 UEFA Nations League match, becoming the second male player to achieve this milestone (after Ali Daei of Iran) and the first in Europe.

Top scorer in National Team history and present (2021-act.)

On June 15, 2021, Ronaldo scored two goals in Portugal's opening match of Euro 2020, a 3-0 win over Hungary in Budapest. This took him to a total of eleven goals at the European Championship, two ahead of Michel Platini as the all-time leading scorer in the competition's history. He also became the first player to score in five European Championships and in eleven consecutive tournaments. The brace made Ronaldo the oldest player to score two goals in a European Championship match, and the oldest player to score for Portugal in a major tournament. On June 23, he scored two penalties in Portugal's 2-2 draw with France in their final group stage match, equaling Daei's record of 109 international goals. On June 27, Portugal was eliminated after losing 1-0 to Belgium in the round of 16. Ronaldo finished the tournament with five goals (tied with Czech Patrik Schick) and one assist, which earned him the Golden Boot. On September 1, Ronaldo scored two headed goals, with the second coming seconds before the full-time whistle, in a 2-1 home win over the Republic of Ireland at the Algarve Stadium, which saw him pass Daei's record of 109 to become the sole record holder.

Player profile

Style of play

A versatile striker, Ronaldo is capable of playing both on the wings and in the center of the field, and, although he is a right-footed player, he is also good with his left foot. He is among the fastest players in the world, with and without the ball. Tactically, Ronaldo underwent several evolutions and changes during his career. While at Sporting and during his first years at United, Cristiano played as a classic right-sided midfielder, where he usually played crosses into the box. In this position, he was able to use his acceleration, change of pace, agility and technical skills to take on opponents in one-on-one situations, and became known for his elaborate dribbling, often demonstrating a variety of tricks and feints, such as the bicycle and so-called "cutbacks", which became his trademark; was also known to be a frequent user of the "elastic".

As Ronaldo matured, he underwent a major physical transformation, developing a muscular body type that allowed him to retain possession of the ball under pressure for longer, and strong legs that allowed him impressive leaping ability. His strength and leaping ability, combined with his elevation, heading accuracy, and height of 1.87 m, gave him a great advantage in winning aerial duels. These attributes allow him to function as a target man in the box, and make him a constant aerial goal threat in the penalty area; consequently, many of his goals have been headers. In conjunction with his increased stamina and sacrifice, his goal scoring ability improved dramatically on the left wing, where he was given the positional freedom to move into the center to finish attacks. He has also increasingly played a creative role for his team, often dropping into the midfield to pick up the ball, participate in setting up plays and creating chances for his teammates, courtesy of his vision and passing ability.

In his final seasons at United, Ronaldo played an even more attacking and central role, functioning as both a number 9 and a second striker, even as an attacking midfielder at times. He became a prolific goalscorer, capable of finishing well both inside the penalty area and from long range, with an accurate and powerful shot. A lethal penalty taker, he also became a set-piece specialist, known for his powerful curling free kicks. When taking them, Ronaldo is known for using the "folha seca" technique, developed by Juninho Pernambucano, which consists of striking the ball with the inside of his foot so that it describes an up-and-down parabola similar to a dry leaf falling from a tree, a metaphor that comes from a goal that the Brazilian "Didi" scored from a free kick against Peru in the 1958 World Cup qualifiers. He also adopts a trademark stance before striking the ball, which sees him position himself in front of the ball with his legs wide apart. Regarding Ronaldo's unique style of taking free kicks, former Manchester United assistant coach Mike Phelan commented: "People used to leave the ball, walk away, run and hit it. He brought a more dynamic show. He puts the ball down, his concentration level is high, he takes a certain amount of steps back so his foot is in the perfect place to hit the ball in the optimum spot. He's the ultimate showman. He has that slight arrogance. When he pulls up those shorts and shows his thighs, he's saying 'All eyes on me' and this ball is going in. He understands the marketing side of it. The way he shows off and places the ball; he knows the world is watching him."

At Real Madrid, Ronaldo continued to play a more attacking role, but his creative and defensive duties became more limited, although not completely diminished. Initially deployed as a center forward by coaches Manuel Pellegrini and José Mourinho, he was later moved back to the left wing, albeit in a free tactical role; this position allowed him to slide into the center at will to get on the end of crosses and score, or draw defenders out of their area with his off-the-ball movements and leave space for his teammates to exploit. Madrid's counter-attacking style of play also allowed him to become a more efficient and consistent player, as evidenced by his record goalscoring marks. While he was praised primarily in the media for being a prolific goalscorer, Ronaldo also demonstrated his ability as an effective creative player in this role. This unique role has been described by pundits as that of a "false", "attacking", or "goal-scoring" winger, as Ronaldo practically functioned as a center forward at times with his constant runs towards the penalty area, despite actually playing on the left wing. From 2013 onwards, already under coach Carlo Ancelotti, Cristiano effectively adapted his style due to the physical effects of aging with increasingly reduced off-ball movement and overall involvement, completing fewer dribbles and passes per game and instead focusing more on creating and scoring from short distances. Since 2017, Ronaldo has adapted his playing style once again to become a free agent center forward under coach Zinedine Zidane, a role in which he continued to excel and maintain a prolific goal scoring record; In this position, he earned praise in the media for his intelligent movement with and without the ball, his positional sense, link-up play and finishing, as well as his ability to lose or anticipate his markers, find space in the box and score with few touches or opportunities.

In his first season at Juventus, Ronaldo continued to play in a variety of different attacking roles under coach Massimiliano Allegri, depending on who he partnered up front. While he had occupied an increasingly attacking role in his final years at Real Madrid, he occasionally played in a free role at Juventus, either as a lone striker or in his trademark role on the left wing in a 4-2-3-1 or 4-3-3 formation, in which he often switched places with Mario Mandžukić. In this role, he was also given permission to drop into midfield, or even drift to the right sector of the field to receive the ball and participate more in setting up plays; thus, in addition to scoring goals himself, he began to take on opponents and create chances for other players more frequently than in his last seasons with Real Madrid. Without the ball, he was also able to create space for teammates with his movements and runs into the box, or finish off chances with his head or feet by getting on the end of his teammates' crosses. At times he also played in an attacking partnership alongside Mandžukić in a 4-3-1-2, 4-4-2 or 3-5-2 formation. He continued to play a similar role in his second season with the club under Maurizio Sarri.

Reception

Cristiano Ronaldo is widely regarded as one of the best players of his generation, alongside Lionel Messi. After winning his first Ballon d'Or in 2008 by a record vote at just 23 years of age, Ronaldo has been subject to several debates as to who is the greatest player of all time. Hailed for his prolific and consistent goalscoring record, he is regarded as a decisive player who is also a game-changer, especially in important situations and where the pressure is high.

Ronaldo is known for his work ethic, impressive fitness, and dedication to improvement in training, as well as being noted as a natural leader. On his longevity and "extraordinary commitment to fitness," Adam Bate of Sky Sports commented, "Dedication plays a big part in staying on top and Ronaldo's approach is perhaps unparalleled within the sport." Although stating that they were aesthetically different players but with the same hunger to score goals, legendary Brazilian striker Ronaldo praised Cristiano's approach to training, arguing that, "There are so few players who take care of their body like he does. I trained because I had to, he does it because he loves it. "His drive and determination to succeed are driven by a desire to be talked about alongside other greats such as Pele and Diego Maradona once he retires. He is credited, along with fellow countryman, coach Jose Mourinho, for inspiring the evolution of Portuguese soccer in the 2010s and 2020s. He has been criticized at times for faking when fouled. He was also occasionally criticized early in his career by manager Alex Ferguson, teammates and the media for being a selfish or overly flamboyant player.

During his career, Ronaldo has also been described as having an "arrogant image" on the field, and Ronaldo claimed that he had become a "victim" because of the way he was portrayed in the media. He is often seen moaning, gesticulating and scowling as he tries to inspire his team to victory, and Ronaldo insists that his competitive nature should not be confused with arrogance. His coaches, teammates and several journalists have said that this reputation has led to an unfair image of him.

Cristiano-Messi rivalry

In popular culture

Cristiano Ronaldo is considered one of the best soccer players, one of the most influential, therefore he has fans all over the world.

Throughout his career, Ronaldo has been included in various international rankings: for example, he ranked second on the Forbes list of the highest paid athletes of the decade, with earnings of €720 million (£615 million) from 2010 to 2019, only boxer Floyd Mayweather Jr. earned more than him. Similarly, Forbes twice ranked him at the top of its list of the world's highest-paid soccer players. In 2016, he became the first soccer player to top the Forbes list of the world's highest-earning athletes, with a total income of $88 million between his salary and sponsorships for the 2015-16 season, he also topped the list for the second year in a row with earnings of $93 million in 2016-17. He is the first soccer player and only the third athlete to earn $1 billion in his career. In addition, Ronaldo is one of the most marketable athletes in the world: SportsPro ranked him as the fifth most marketable athlete in 2012 and the eighth most marketable athlete in 2013. In May 2014 the sports market research company Repucom named him the most marketable and most recognized soccer player in the world. In 2014 the Times magazine included him in its Time 100 list as one of the 100 most influential people in the world. ESPN named the soccer player as the world's most famous athlete in 2016, 2017, 2018 and 2019.

Although fanaticism for the player has its focus in Portugal, Madrid and Manchester, his soccer career has been recognized on numerous occasions. Several surveys place him among the best players in history. In addition to the various prizes and awards given by official bodies and sports publications around the world, Ronaldo received two important recognitions: On June 17, 2015 an astronomical research organization composed of 16 nations named the newly discovered Cosmos Redshift 7 galaxy in his honor, likewise, on March 29, 2017 the airport near his hometown was officially renamed in tribute to his career as Cristiano Ronaldo International Airport. He has also been awarded by the Portuguese presidency, when in 2004 he was awarded the distinction of Officer of the Order of the Infante Don Enrique and in 2014 he was awarded the Grand Officer of the Order of the Infante Don Enrique, both for his career.

His influence on and off the field has been such that he has become an example to follow and a source of inspiration for professional soccer players and soccer fans. In the streets of different parts of the world there are murals, paintings, statues and drawings of the Portuguese. In addition, poems, songs and letters have been written and dedicated to him.

Statistics

Clubs

*Updated as of the last game played on **May 7, 2022**.*

Source: CeroACero - Transfermarkt - BDFutbol -SharkScores. - ESPN Deportes.

Portugal National Team

*Updated as of the last game played on **June 5, 2021**.*

Source: FFP - ESPN Deportes. - Transfermarkt. - RSSSF. - People

Individual records and achievements

Among his achievements, some stand out for his high scoring record as a professional. In 2013, the player scored 69 goals in a calendar year, being the best mark of the mentioned period worldwide and his own. Achieved with Real Madrid C. F. (59 goals) and with the Portugal national soccer team (10 goals), they contributed to his winning the FIFA Ballon d'Or, the second in his career. The record included seven *hat-tricks* and fifteen braces. The following season, 2014-15, he scored 61 goals in 54 games, averaging 1.13 goals per game, to become the Madrid player with the most goals in a season in the club's history and the highest scoring season of his entire professional career. Six braces, six *hat-tricks*, a hat-*trick*, a hat-trick and a poker stood out among the goals.

Divided by competition, it was in Europe's top club competition, the Champions League, where he signed some of his most important achievements. In the aforementioned 2013-14 season, he reached the absolute record of goals in a single edition in the entire history of the tournament with 17 goals in 11 games, yielding a scoring average of 1.55 per game. It was also the highest figure achieved by any player in a European competition, equaling Radamel Falcao's 2011 Europa League record. He managed to score at least one goal in every stage of the tournament. Those numbers took him along with the rest of the seasons and UEFA competitions to a career tally of 108 goals, the highest ever achieved by a footballer. Of these, 106 were in the Champions League and 2 in the European Super Cup, while the club and stadium where he scored the most goals were the aforementioned Real Madrid C. F. (90 goals) and the Santiago Bernabeu Stadium (47 goals). His favorite "victim" was Fußball-Club Bayern, against whom he scored 9 goals.

In Spain, he set a new absolute record for goals in the start of the 2014-15 League, scoring fifteen goals in eight matchdays, the highest figure achieved by any player in Spanish competition and surpassing the previous record, achieved by Esteban Echevarría in the 1943-44 season of fourteen goals in eight matchdays. The record continued to increase four more matchdays, scoring a total of twenty goals in twelve matchdays, surpassing Isidro Lángara's record of the 1935-36 season with sixteen goals in ten matchdays. The record was achieved after scoring at least one goal in each of the eleven matches played (he missed one match due to injury), also setting a new club record for consecutive matches scoring in La Liga, for a total of twenty goals and surpassing the previous record of thirteen goals in seven matches held by Ferenc Puskás in 1959-60 and 1960-61.

In the 2014-15 season, he set a new personal record by managing to score twenty goals during twelve consecutive matches in all competitions in play. The streak came to a halt on matchday four of the Champions League, where he failed to score on Liverpool Football Club's visit to Madrid.

With three titles, Cristiano Ronaldo is the player who has won the UEFA Best Player Award in Europe the most times.

On June 15, 2018, he became the fourth player in World Cup history to score goals in four different editions of the tournament, joining Pele, Uwe Seeler and Miroslav Klose. On April 20, 2019, he became the first player to be champion in Europe's top three leagues, England's Premier League, Spain's La Liga and Italy's Serie A.

Finally, it is important to note that between national and club teams, Cristiano has scored for 169 teams (123 clubs and 46 national teams).

Private life

Cristiano Ronaldo speaks Portuguese, English and Spanish, while he owes his name to his parents' admiration for the actor and later U.S. President Ronald Reagan. His father, José Dinis Aveiro, died of a renal crisis due to alcohol on September 7, 2005, when Cristiano was twenty years old and was concentrating with the national team. Hours later, he met with the coach of the Portuguese team to inform him of his intention to play the match against Russia for the qualification to the 2006 World Cup. After the engagement, the coach of his then club, Alex Ferguson, allowed him to return to his hometown for the funeral, so he missed the match against Manchester City, one of the rare occasions in which he has missed a match for extra-sporting reasons.

After two World Cup qualification matches, he traveled to Indonesia to raise funds for the 2004 Indian Ocean tsunami. He met with Vice President Jusuf Kalla and East Timor President Xanana Gusmão to make a contribution of $120,000. Throughout his career, gender actions were closely linked to his life, being very active and contributing to the social cause and in favor of health and development. He auctioned the Golden Boot achieved in 2011 to raise funds for the children of Gaza, in Palestine after the Gaza Strip was heavily bombed by Israeli troops, while through numerous associations and with donations, to cite other examples, the Portuguese helps to the extent allowed by his agenda. It is not for nothing that he overcame a near-fatal heart operation in his childhood, which is also one of the reasons for his actions and his Catholic religion, which he also professes.

On July 4, 2010, a few days after Portugal's defeat in the 2010 World Cup, he announced through social networks that he was the father of a baby boy, Cristiano Jr, who was born in the state of California in the United States. It was agreed with the mother that his identity would be kept secret and the child would remain under her guardianship. Subsequently, he followed a similar process with a surrogate pregnancy in 2017 through which he became a father again, this time of twins, Eva and Mateo. In between, he maintained a relationship with Russian model Irina Shayk until the beginning of 2015 and, after spending a period without a stable relationship known, at least to public opinion, he began a relationship with Spanish-Argentine Georgina Rodriguez in the summer of 2016. Rodriguez and Ronaldo were seen together in public for the first time in

November 2016, when they went to Disneyland Paris. Just five months after the birth of the twins, his girlfriend Georgina gave birth on November 12, 2017 to the footballer's fourth child, Alana Martina. In October 2021 it was made public that he was going to become a father of twins for the second time. In April 2022, the birth of his second daughter, and the death of her twin brother, was made public.

His successes and media impact led him to perform alternative jobs as a model for major international brands and firms and as an entrepreneur, complementary to his sports career.

Controversies

Ronaldo and another man were investigated by the British Crown Prosecution Service after a 2005 rape allegation was made by two women. Within days, the two women withdrew their allegation and Scotland Yard issued a statement declaring that there was insufficient evidence for a prosecution.

In April 2017, it was reported that Ronaldo was under investigation for another rape allegation by the Las Vegas Police Department that originated in 2009. Documents surfaced claiming that Cristiano Ronaldo allegedly paid a woman US $375,000 in a confidentiality agreement. Ronaldo and his lawyers issued a lengthy statement denying all the allegations, describing them as an "intentional smear campaign" with parts significantly "altered and/or completely fabricated," a claim that Der Spiegel categorically refuted. Finally, on July 22, 2019, the complaint was dismissed - due to the absence of evidence - by the Clark County District

Attorney's Office, Las Vegas, leaving the Portuguese footballer free to be charged and tried.

Judicial process

Cristiano Ronaldo's case actually began in 2004, when the player, already in the elite, entrusted himself to the 'Mendes method' to manage his advertising income. The tax scheme used during this time to allegedly avoid paying taxes, has ended up with the footballer before the Spanish Justice.In the summer of 2004, after signing for Manchester United, Ronaldo allegedly created an offshore structure to avoid paying taxes on his advertising income. His worldwide earnings (except for those in the UK) were held in Tollin, a company with no employees or real activity in the tax haven of the British Virgin Islands. A week before finalizing his signing with Real Madrid, on December 20, 2008, Cristiano Ronaldo changed this alleged scheme. While in the United Kingdom he kept his income from image rights in a company based in Manchester, in Spain he did not create any company for that purpose: all the money went to the Caribbean. In the context of the end of the Beckham Law and the tax inspections of other clients of Jorge Mendes, Ronaldo filed his 2014 income tax return. Despite having already invoiced 150 million for advertising between 2009 and 2014, he was taxed for 22.7 and paid only 5.6 million for Personal Income Tax.On December 3, 2015, the Treasury opened proceedings against Ronaldo for possible irregularities in his tax returns for the years 2011, 2012 and 2013. Later, they would extend the inquiries to the fiscal year corresponding to 2014.A year after Hacienda began its inspection, the newspaper El Mundo and its partners at

EIC revealed Ronaldo's alleged scheme to divert income to a tax haven.Hacienda completed its investigation in May 2017 with the conclusion that Ronaldo defrauded €14.7 million in taxes between 2011 and 2014. Two weeks later, the Prosecutor's Office denounced him for four tax offenses. The judge admitted the complaint for processing and summoned him to testify on Monday, July 31, in the capacity of investigated.

As pointed out by the Union of Tax Technicians, the Portuguese footballer could have incurred in a tax offense in 2011, and in two other aggravated tax offenses in 2012 and 2013, as the allegedly defrauded fees exceeded 600,000 euros. These two offenses carry prison sentences of two to six years for each of them.However, the judge could apply the highly qualified mitigating factor of extemporaneous regularization introduced in the Penal Code in 2013 and reduce the penalty to half or a quarter of each tax offense if the player acknowledges the facts and pays the allegedly defrauded quotas, interest and fines within a maximum period of two months from the court summons as investigated.Likewise, Gestha considers that Ronaldo's tax advisors should be investigated as necessary cooperators in the alleged tax offenses, especially after the revelations of Football Leaks, which alerted about the emails that the player's lawyers and the representative's lawyers exchanged.

In June 2018, Ronaldo received a two-year suspended prison sentence and a fine of €18.8 million, which was later reduced to €16.8 million upon reaching an agreement with the Spanish authorities. The sentence can be served on probation, without any jail time, as long as he does not reoffend.

Other books by United Library

https://campsite.bio/unitedlibrary

Lightning Source UK Ltd.
Milton Keynes UK
UKHW021959071222
413550UK00010B/664